LOVE
Colouring Book

LOVE
Colouring Book

This edition published in 2024 by Arcturus Publishing Limited
26/27 Bickels Yard, 151–153 Bermondsey Street,
London SE1 3HA

Copyright © Arcturus Holdings Limited

All rights reserved. No part of this publication may be reproduced, stored in a retrieval system, or transmitted, in any form or by any means, electronic, mechanical, photocopying, recording, or otherwise, without prior written permission in accordance with the provisions of the Copyright Act 1956 (as amended). Any person or persons who do any unauthorized act in relation to this publication may be liable to criminal prosecution and civil claims for damages.

ISBN: 978-1-78950-784-3
CH007281NT
Supplier 29, Date 0124, PI00007547

Printed in China

Created for children 10+

Introduction

You'll find that love is all around when you open this colouring book packed with images of hearts, flowers, romantic abstracts and dreamy mandalas. Let your emotions take centre stage as you focus on adding colour to the gorgeous patterns and discover a tranquil, feel-good state of mind.

Like a surprise bunch of flowers or a lighthouse in a stormy sea, these pages offer a happy refuge from an often demanding and stress-filled world.

So take the plunge and discover your inner softie. All you need is love (and a set of coloured pens or pencils).

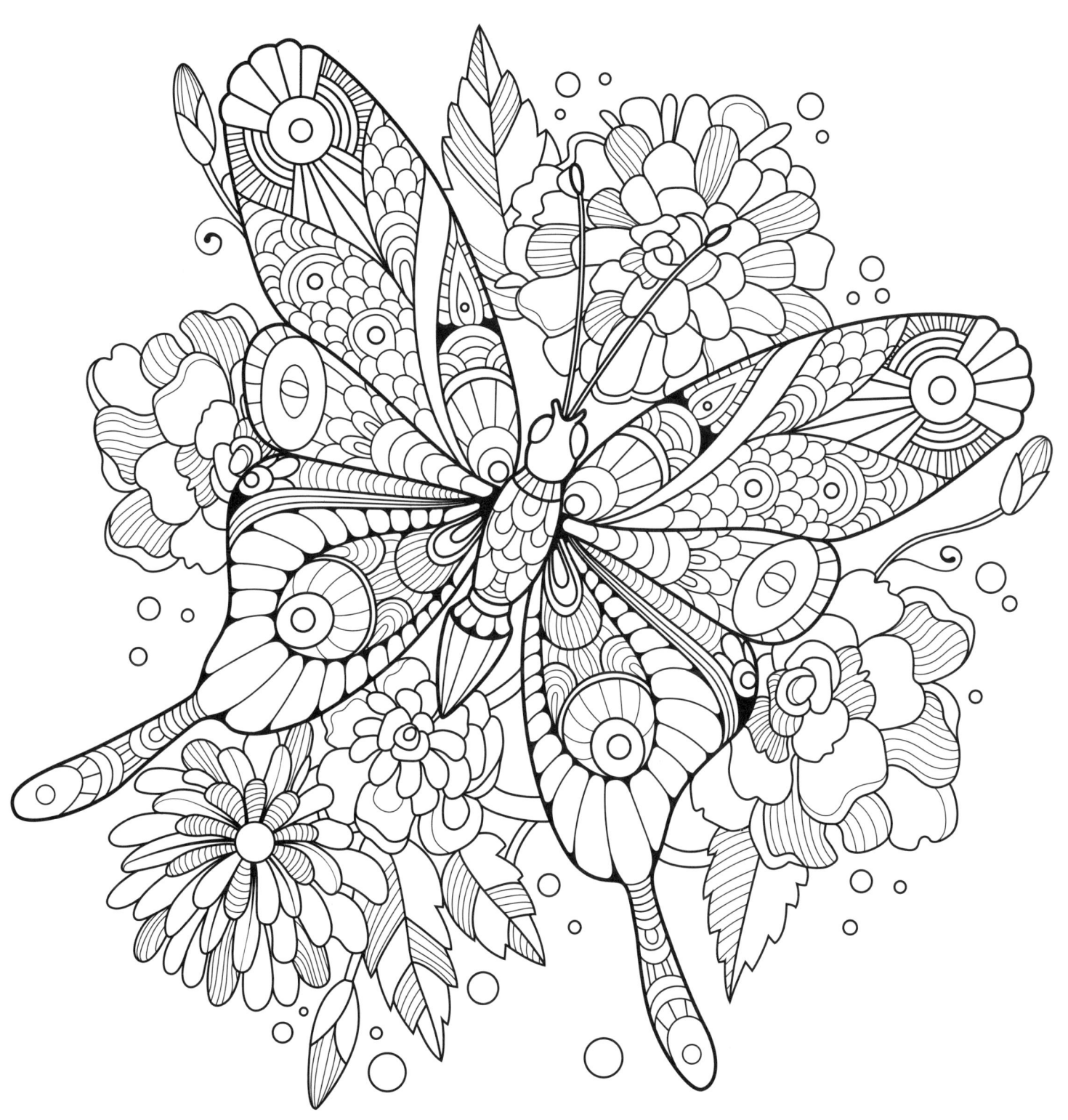

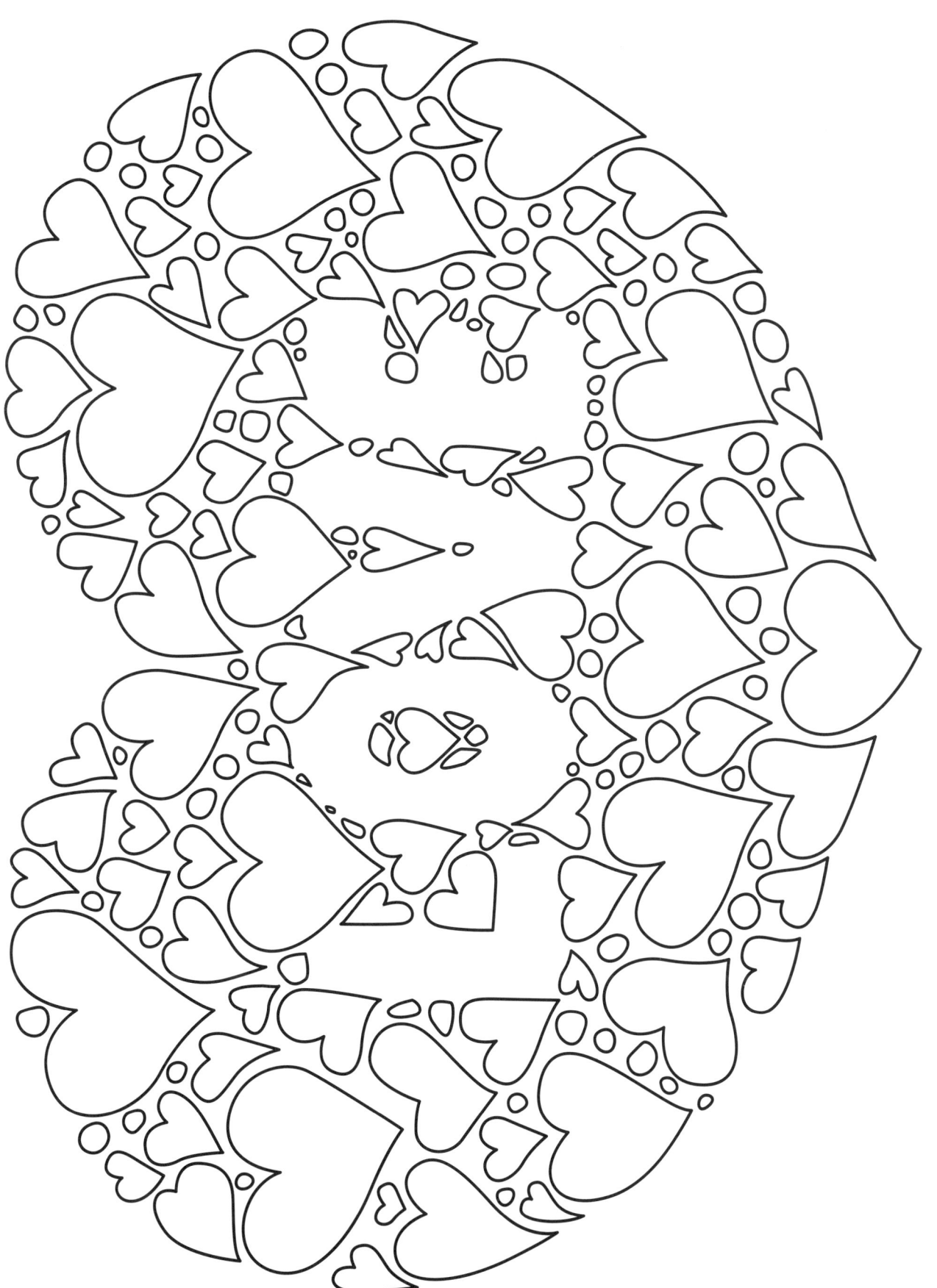